Nebraska Wildlife

Animals & Mammals

Billy Grinslott & Kinsey Marie Books

ISBN - 9781965098936

Chipmunks are found in many areas. Chipmunks are small members of the squirrel family. They like to eat nuts and seeds. Chipmunks are most active during the day, especially at dawn and dusk. They have pouches inside of their cheeks so they can carry food. They are very friendly and will take food from your hand. Chipmunks need about 15 hours of sleep per day. The smallest chipmunk species is Tamias minimus, which is found throughout North America.

There are many squirrels in the wild. You may see a red or gray squirrel. The most popular is the gray squirrel. Squirrels are very acrobatic and can climb trees. Their favorite food is acorns. Squirrels hide their food in many small stashes and can find more than 90% of them later. Squirrels are fast and can run up a tree at 12 miles per hour. Newborn squirrels are blind, deaf, and hairless, and rely on their mother until they mature.

Ground squirrels are primarily active during the day and rest at night. They are known for their complex burrow systems with multiple entrances, providing shelter and escape routes from predators. Many ground squirrel species hibernate during the winter months, preparing for dormancy by gaining weight and storing food. They have good senses of vision, smell, and touch, and communicate using alarm calls.

Flying Squirrels don't fly like birds. They don't have wings. They have skin that is attached to their legs. When they jump from a tree, they spread their legs out and glide through the air. Most glides are 30 feet from tree to tree. But they can glide up to 150 feet.

Groundhogs or woodchucks are the largest member of the squirrel family. Groundhogs get their name because of their big bodies, and they live underground. Groundhogs are skilled climbers and swimmers. Groundhogs are true hibernators, sleeping for up to six months. Groundhog Day is where Punxsutawney Phil predicts how long winter will last.

Prairie dogs live in family groups called coteries, which are made up of one male, several females, and their young. Their vocabulary is more advanced than any other animal language. They got their name because they live on the prairies and their warning calls which sound like dog barks. They build mounds around their den to keep water out. Prairie dogs are small burrowing mammals that are related to squirrels.

Pocket gophers are burrowing rodents and are known for their digging activities and unique adaptations for underground life. They have very sharp claws for digging. They create complex underground tunnel systems. Their fur-lined cheek pouches, or pockets, are used to store and transport food, like roots, tubers, and grasses, back to their burrows. They can turn their cheek pouches inside out for grooming purposes. Their tails are highly sensitive and act as feelers to help them navigate the dark tunnels, even when backing up.

There are many types of rabbits in the wild. The most common is the cottontail. Rabbits are cute, friendly, and fun to watch. Many people have rabbits for pets. They have soft fluffy fur. They are called cottontails because they have a white fluffy tail that looks like a cotton ball.

The hare is bigger than a rabbit with longer ears and legs. Their longs legs help them to run fast. They are agile and faster than most rabbits. Hares have excellent hearing and vision. Hares have large ears and eyes that are positioned on the sides of their head, giving them a wide field of vision. Hares can change color. Hares have the ability to change color depending on the season and their surroundings.

Pee-ewe what is that stinky critter with the big bushy tail. It smells bad. Skunks are normally curious and friendly unless you scare them. If you scare them, they will flip their bushy tale at you and spray you with a smelly potion and it stinks. Skunks spray a smelly, sulfur-based liquid from their anal glands as a defense mechanism. The spray can cause eye irritation and temporary blindness. Skunks are highly adaptable and can thrive in many different environments. Skunks have strong forefeet and long claws for digging. Skunks live in dens.

Opossums or possums have strong tails and can hang from trees. One trick that a possum has, is when it feels danger is it will play dead. It will lay there and not move. Possums have white to gray face hair. Possums like to eat wood ticks. They are also immune to snakebites. Opossums are susceptible to frostbite because their hands and tails are not protected by fur. Opossums are marsupials, which means they have pouches for their young, like kangaroos and koalas.

Raccoons like to come out at night. Their eyes are made so they can see in the dark. Raccoons are highly intelligent and can solve problems. They can learn to open doors, trash cans, and other containers. They are called masked bandits because they like to raid and eat out of trash cans at night. Raccoons can survive in many environments.

Beavers use their teeth to cut and knock down trees. They build dams with them to block water, so they have a place to live and swim. They also eat wood. Beavers can stay underwater for about 8 minutes. Beavers slap their tails on the water to indicate danger. Beavers are the largest rodents in North America.

Otters have the thickest fur of any animal. The otter is one of the few mammals that use tools, like rocks to break thing open. A group of otters resting together is called a raft.

Otters primarily rely on their sense of touch, whiskers, and forepaws, in murky waters to locate food. Otters have built in pouches of loose skin under their forearms to stash extra food when diving.

Badgers have elongated heads, small ears, and black and white faces. Badgers live underground with other family members. Badgers are very social and live in groups. A badger den or sett can be centuries old and are used by many generations of badgers. Badgers are very territorial, it's best not to bother them is you see one. A group of badgers is called a cete, though they are often called clans. Badgers are largely nocturnal but reduce their activity during periods of cold weather.

The American Mink lives across most of North America and is a cat sized. Mink are very skilled climbers and swimmers. They prefer to keep to themselves. They communicate using odors, visual signals, and other sounds. They purr when they're happy. Mink are agile swimmers, and they often dive to find food

Mallard ducks are by far the most recognizable and popular ducks in the world. They live in just about every area of North America. Their estimated population is around 19 million birds. The male is easily recognizable from its white neck ring and green neck and head. The female Mallard has between five to 14 light green eggs. Most ducks don't have green eggs, so this makes them unique. The male Mallard is called a drake and the female a hen. Female Mallards quack. Males don't quack, instead they produce deeper, raspier one- and two-note calls. They can also make rattling sounds by rubbing their bills against their flight feathers.

Canada Geese are the most sought after and abundant goose in North America. They live in many places. Canada geese can travel 1,500 miles in a day if the weather permits. Canada geese migrate every year. They fly in a V-formation, which allows them to travel long distances without stopping, as they can switch positions and conserve energy. Canada geese are known for their distinctive honk and are sometimes called Canadian honkers.

Ringed Neck Pheasants are one of the most sought-after birds in North America. They are found throughout most of Northern America and Canada. Ring-necked pheasants are not native to the US. Instead, they were brought here from Asia in the 1880's. South Dakota is one of the best places to find Pheasants.

The bobwhite quail has the largest range of any game bird in America. Bobwhite quail are the most common species of quail, the bobwhite is often referred to as the number one game bird of the eastern and southern United States. At night, they roost on the ground in a circle, with their tails pointed inward and heads outward, which helps them conserve heat and stay alert to potential predators.

The Wild Turkey is a large, bird that is native to North America. It is the heaviest bird in the United States and can weigh up to 24 pounds. Only male turkey's gobble. Wild turkeys can fly. Wild turkeys sleep in trees. Their heads can change colors. You can tell a turkey's emotions by the color of their heads. Colors can change from red to blue to white, depending on how excited or calm they are. You can find wild turkeys in just about every state in America.

Nebraska has grouse, specifically two species: greater prairie chickens and sharp-tailed grouse. They are primarily found in the Sandhills region of Nebraska. Grouse are interesting birds known for their unique drumming displays. They flap or rotate their wings, and it sounds like drums. Prairie grouse can be an underutilized game species, especially compared to pheasants, quail, and doves.

Bald eagles are large birds, with females up to 43 inches long and weighing up to 13 pounds. Their wingspan can be up to 7 feet wide. Bald eagles build the largest nests of any bird, up to 13 feet wide and weighing more than half a ton. Bald eagles aren't actually bald. The name bald eagle comes from the old English word piebald bird, which meant white-headed bird. Bald eagles have the best eyesight of any bird. A bald eagle can see up to three miles away, which is about four to five times farther than a human. They can also see small details like an ant on the ground from great distances.

Bobcats are named for their short, bobbed tails with white tips. They have similar markings to lynxes but are much smaller. Bobcats live in a variety of habitats. Bobcats are skilled at leaping and can run up to 30 miles per hour.

The cougar has a number of different names, it's also known as the mountain lion. They are the fourth largest cat in the world. The cougar has the largest range of any wild cat in the North America. A cougar can jump upward 18 feet from a sitting position. They can leap up to 30 feet horizontally. Cougars cannot roar like a lion, but they can make calls like a human scream.

The Kit or swift foxes are native to much of the western United States and northern Mexico. Kit foxes are the smallest foxes in North America, weighing only about five pounds.. Despite their slender size, they have large ears to help aid their hearing and to dissipate heat. Kit foxes are mainly active at night and resting in their dens during the day. kit foxes can survive without fresh water, by getting all their fluids from their food.

Red foxes have excellent hearing, allowing them to hear rodents digging underground from miles away. When afraid, red foxes grin or look like they are smiling. Red foxes front paws have five toes, while their hind feet only have four. Foxes dig underground dens where they raise their kits and hide from predators. A group of foxes is called a skulk or a leash. Babys are called kits and females are called vixens.

The coyote is bigger than a fox weighing between 20 and 45 pounds. Eastern coyotes are part wolf. Coyotes are great for pest control. They like to eat mice and rats. They can adapt and live almost anywhere, even in the city. Coyotes are very smart and have been observed learning and following traffic signals in some cities. They have a yip type of call when they communicate with each other. Coyotes are found in all the United States, except Hawaii.

Black bears are the smallest members of the bear family in North America. Black Bears love to eat sweet things like berries, fruits, and vegetables. They are good climbers and fast runners. They are excellent swimmers and can paddle at least a mile and a half in freshwater. They usually sleep for long periods of time and hibernate during the winter. They typically try to stay away from people unless they find food in the area.

There are several types of antelopes, this one is known as the pronghorn. Antelopes have extremely developed senses which help them detect danger. They are quick runners and can run up to 60 mph. They can maintain high speeds for longer periods of time than cheetahs. They all like to live in herds. Antelopes don't outrun other animals. They out maneuver them. They can twist and turn very quickly. They are related to cows, sheep, and goats.

The whitetail deer is the most popular deer in North America. Whitetail deer have good eyesight and hearing. They can detect small sounds from a quarter of a mile away. Only male deer grow antlers, which are shed each year. Whitetail deer are good swimmers and will use large streams and lakes to escape predators. A young deer is called a fawn, a male is a buck, and a female is called a doe. They are the most common deer species and live everywhere in North America.

Mule deer get their name because of their mule like ears. Male deer are called bucks and females are does. Males grow new antlers every year. They can run 45 miles per hour. Mule deer can jump 2 feet high and up to 15 feet in distance. They are bigger than whitetail deer and prefer living in the mountain areas. A mule deer's eyes are located on the side of its head, providing 310 degrees of vision. Mule deer have great night vision.

Elk are the second largest members of the deer family. Bulls can weigh up to 1,100 lbs. Elk antlers can grow up to an inch per day. They can run 40 miles per hour and outrun horses. Elk have a good sense of hearing and can swivel their ears back and forth. Elk have eyes on the sides of their heads and can see in every direction except directly in front or behind. They make a cool bugling sound when communicating with other elk. It's fun to listen to them.

The bighorn sheep is part of the sheep family and likes to live in mountainous areas. Females are called ewes and males are called rams. They are called rams because they like to use their horns to slam into things. Their horn size is a symbol of how high they rank in the herd. The bigger their horns are, the higher they rank. Their large curled horns that can weigh up to 30 pounds. Bighorn sheep are excellent climbers and can stand on ledges as narrow as 2 inches.

Originally from Asia, sika deer were introduced to the USA to be used for hunting. Sika means deer in Japanese. Sika deer can jump up to 30 feet in one bound. They have at least 10 different vocalizations, including soft whistles, loud screams, horse-like neighs, goat-like bleating and alarm calls. They are primarily nocturnal (active at night) but can be seen in daylight hours if they are comfortable with their habitat. Sika deer are being a medium-sized member of the deer family.

While not a common occurrence, moose sightings do happen in Nebraska, particularly in the Panhandle region. These moose are believed to have traveled from Colorado and Wyoming, following river corridors Moose are built for cold areas and like living in cold regions with snow. Moose are the largest members of the deer family. Moose are huge and weigh up to 1500 pounds. Moose love water and are good swimmers. Moose have poor eyesight but compensate with a good sense of smell and hearing. At 5 days old they can outrun a person.

The North American Bison and Buffalo are sometimes confused as the same animal, but they are not. Bison have long hair on their backs, front, and a long beard. Bison are bigger than buffalo. They are the largest mammal in North America and weigh up to 2,000 pounds. Bison can run up to 35 miles per hour. They can jump 6 feet vertically and more than 7 feet horizontally. Bison calves are nicknamed red dogs, because of their orange-red color at birth.

Fun Facts about Nebraska Animals

1 - The state animal of Nebraska is the white-tailed deer. It was officially designated as the state mammal in 1981.

2 - Pronghorns antelopes are the fastest land mammal in North America, capable of reaching speeds of up to 60 miles per hour.

3 - Nebraska has a wide variety of wildlife, including over 450 bird species, 95 mammal species, 106 fish species, 61 amphibians and reptiles.

4 - Elk are Nebraska's largest big game species, while bighorn sheep have been reintroduced to certain areas.

5 - Moose are the largest members of the deer family.

6 - Bison were nearly wiped out in the 1800s but still roam in managed herds throughout Nebraska.

7 - There are more than 95 mammals are found in Nebraska, but many are small and seldom seen.

8 - The American bison is one of the largest and most recognizable mammals in Nebraska. They can weigh up to 2 thousand pounds.

Author Page

Billy Grinslott & Kinsey Marie Books

Copyright, All Rights Reserved

ISBN - 9781965098936

Thanks

www.ingramcontent.com/pod-product-compliance
Lightning Source LLC
Chambersburg PA
CBHW042151290326
41934CB00002BA/96

9781965098936